Pokémon

Beginner's Guide

Josh Gregory

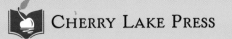
CHERRY LAKE PRESS

Published in the United States of America by Cherry Lake Publishing Group
Ann Arbor, Michigan
www.cherrylakepublishing.com

Reading Adviser: Beth Walker Gambro, MS, Ed., Reading Consultant, Yorkville, IL

Photo Credits: © sharppy / Shutterstock, 17

Cherry Lake Press is an imprint of Cherry Lake Publishing Group.

Library of Congress Cataloging-in-Publication Data

Names: Gregory, Josh, author.
Title: Pokémon : beginner's guide / by Josh Gregory.
Description: Ann Arbor, Michigan : Cherry Lake Press, [2023] | Series: 21st century skills innovation library. Unofficial guides | Includes bibliographical references and index. | Audience: Grades 4-6 | Summary: "With each new game in the long-running Pokémon series, a new generation of players is introduced to the simple, yet irresistible concept of catching colorful monsters and battling them against other players. In this book, readers will learn about the history of this classic game series and find out what they need to get started on their own Pokémon-collecting journey. Includes table of contents, author biography, sidebars, glossary, index, and informative backmatter" — Provided by publisher.
Identifiers: LCCN 2023002152 (print) | LCCN 2023002153 (ebook) | ISBN 9781668927953 (library binding) | ISBN 9781668929001 (paperback) | ISBN 9781668930472 (epub) | ISBN 9781668933435 (kindle edition) | ISBN 9781668931950 (pdf)
Subjects: LCSH: Pokémon (Game) — Juvenile literature.
Classification: LCC GV1469.35.P63 G75 2023 (print) | LCC GV1469.35.P63 (ebook) | DDC 794.8 — dc23/eng/20230119
LC record available at https://lccn.loc.gov/2023002152
LC ebook record available at https://lccn.loc.gov/2023002153

Cherry Lake Publishing Group would like to acknowledge the work of the Partnership for 21st Century Learning, a Network of Battelle for Kids. Please visit http://www.battelleforkids.org/networks/p21 for more information.

Printed in the United States of America

Note from publisher: Websites change regularly, and their future contents are outside of our control.
Supervise children when conducting any recommended online searches for extended learning opportunities.

Josh Gregory is the author of more than 200 books for kids. He has written about everything from animals to technology to history. A graduate of the University of Missouri–Columbia, he currently lives in Chicago, Illinois.

Contents

CHAPTER 1

Creating a Classic

No matter who you are or what you're interested in, chances are good that you have heard of Pokémon. There are Pokémon TV shows and movies. There are Pokémon card games, toys, comic books, and even a live stage musical. You'll find Pokémon characters on everything from clothes and snacks to bedsheets and toothbrushes. There are Pokémon just about everywhere you look! But it wasn't always that way. The entire Pokémon craze all started with a simple video game about collecting strange little monsters.

The main Pokémon video game series was created by a **development** team called Game Freak. The company was led by a game designer named Satoshi Tajiri. As a child, one of Tajiri's favorite hobbies had been collecting as many different kinds of bugs as he could find outside.

He was so dedicated to it that his friends even called him "Dr. Bug."

When Nintendo's portable Game Boy was released in 1989, players had to connect two systems together using a cable if they wanted to compete head-to-head in games like *Tetris*. When Tajiri saw this, he imagined a game where players could collect bug-like creatures and send them back and forth between Game Boys using the cable.

Today, just about everyone on Earth knows what a Pokémon is.

From Magazines to Megahits

Game Freak did not start out as a video game development company. Satoshi Tajiri launched *Game Freak* as a self-published video game magazine in 1983. He was soon joined by Ken Sugimori, an illustrator who decided to help work on the magazine after reading a copy at a newsstand. It was only in 1989 that Tajiri decided to start making games.

With Sugimori and other friends, Tajiri formed Game Freak and began working on the first Pokémon games as well as titles such as *Yoshi* and *Mario & Wario* for Nintendo. Sugimori ended up creating the designs for all 151 of the original Pokémon. This means his decision to do artwork for a little-known underground magazine eventually led to the chance to create characters known around the world by countless people!

Tajiri first presented this idea to Nintendo in 1990. Not everyone at Nintendo thought that Tajiri's idea would make for a fun game. But legendary game designer Shigeru Miyamoto, the creator of *Super Mario Bros., Donkey Kong,* and *The Legend of Zelda,* was intrigued by it. He convinced Nintendo to allow Game Freak to start working on the game. He also came up with the idea of having different versions of the game, each with different creatures. This would encourage players to trade with friends who had different versions of the game.

Game Freak spent six years developing Tajiri's idea into a completed game. The results were *Pocket Monsters: Red* and *Pocket Monsters: Green*. The games were a huge success upon their release in Japan, and two years later they were released in the United States as

Super Mario 64 is among the many landmark video games designed by Shigeru Miyamoto.

Pokémon Red and *Pokémon Blue*. The name "Pokémon" came from the Japanese style of abbreviating terms by combining parts of words together. The games immediately became the fastest-selling games in the history of the Game Boy, with millions of copies flying off the shelves.

In *Pokémon Red* and *Pokémon Blue*, players take control of a young Pokémon trainer and set off on a journey to explore the world and catch as many

The earliest Pokémon games had very simple, blocky graphics.

The latest Pokémon games are a major visual upgrade over the originals.

different kinds of Pokémon as they can. The player's goal is to defeat other Pokémon trainers in Pokémon battles and become the world's top trainer. This basic formula has stayed the same for the entire history of Pokémon games. With each new game, a new group of players discovers what makes catching Pokémon so fun and addictive. People who played the original games as kids are now adults, and they share their love of Pokémon with their own kids, passing down the series from one **generation** to the next.

CHAPTER 2

Many Ways to Play

Today, there are dozens of games in the Pokémon series. Altogether, they have sold hundreds of millions of copies. Meanwhile, Pokémon mobile apps have been downloaded more than one billion times.

There are Pokémon games available for every Nintendo system to be released since the series began. This means you have a lot of choices available if you want to start playing Pokémon games for the first time.

The main Pokémon series is made up of **roleplaying games** (RPGs) released mostly for Nintendo's handheld systems. These games are typically released two at a time, just like *Pokémon Red* and *Pokémon Blue*. Each set of new games is referred to as a "generation" or "gen" by fans of the series. Sometimes a third game in the same generation will also be released a year or two after the first two.

In each generation, the games are mostly the same: they have the same storyline, the same controls, and the same basic gameplay systems. What changes is mainly the **species** of Pokémon available in each version. Dedicated players carefully consider which Pokémon they want to collect before choosing a version. Some mega-fans even seek out all the versions to make sure they don't miss out.

At the start of *Pokémon Scarlet* and *Pokémon Violet*, players get to choose between Sprigatito, the Grass Cat Pokémon; Fuecoco, the Fire Croc Pokémon; and Quaxly, the Duckling Pokémon.

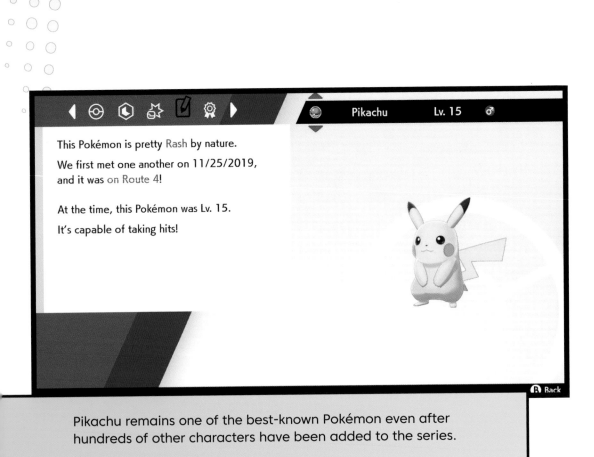

This Pokémon is pretty Rash by nature.
We first met one another on 11/25/2019, and it was on Route 4!

At the time, this Pokémon was Lv. 15.
It's capable of taking hits!

Pikachu   Lv. 15   ♂

Ⓑ Back

Pikachu remains one of the best-known Pokémon even after hundreds of other characters have been added to the series.

In addition to *Pokémon Red* and *Pokémon Blue*, the first generation got an additional version called *Pokémon Yellow* in 1998. This version gave players the chance to start the game with Pikachu, a type of Pokémon that became very popular because it plays a big role in the *Pokémon* cartoon series. Since then, Pikachu has served as a mascot for the series.

The second generation came with *Pokémon Gold* and *Pokémon Silver*, released in 1999 for the Game Boy Color. A third version called *Pokémon Crystal* was released a year later.

The third generation started with *Pokémon Ruby* and *Pokémon Sapphire* in 2002 and continued with *Pokémon Emerald* in 2004. This generation was playable on the Game Boy Advance system.

A New Coat of Paint

Sometimes older Pokémon generations are remade in updated versions for newer game systems. For example, in 2004, *Pokémon FireRed* and *Pokémon LeafGreen* were released for the Game Boy Advance. These games were remakes of the first two Pokémon games. They feature the same stories and sets of available Pokémon as the original games. However, because they are on the Game Boy Advance, they have higher quality graphics. They also include additional features and areas to explore that weren't in the original games.

These kinds of remakes have become common in the series. The first four Pokémon generations have all received remake versions so far. These new versions are popular with fans who want to revisit old favorite Pokémon games on the latest gaming systems.

The Nintendo DS was the first system to get multiple new Pokémon generations. Generation four kicked off with *Pokémon Diamond* and *Pokémon Pearl* in 2006 and concluded with *Pokémon Platinum* in 2008. Then, in 2010, *Pokémon Black* and *Pokémon White* were released, beginning the fifth generation. Instead of the usual third game, Game Freak followed these games up with direct sequels for the first time in Pokémon history. *Pokémon Black 2* and *Pokémon White 2* were released in 2012.

Pokémon Sword and *Pokémon Shield* introduced explorable open-world areas to the series for the first time.

After that, each generation so far has only had two games. *Pokémon X* and *Pokémon Y* were released for the Nintendo 3DS in 2013, making up generation six. Generation seven, made up of *Pokémon Sun* and *Pokémon Moon*, was released for the 3DS in 2016.

The eighth generation, released in 2019 for the Nintendo Switch, marked the first time a main series Pokémon game was playable on a home console and not just a handheld system. Longtime fans were thrilled to play *Pokémon Sword* and *Pokémon Shield* on big TVs, then pick up their Switch systems and take the games on the go.

Generation nine was also released for the Nintendo Switch. *Pokémon Scarlet* and *Pokémon Violet* were released in 2022, and they introduced the first fully open world to the series. This meant players could wander around in any direction as they sought out new Pokémon for their collections, rather than following a certain path through the game's storyline.

So which generation of Pokémon should you play first? Whichever one you want! Simply choose one that's available for a gaming system you own and dive in. Each one will give you knowledge that can help if you decide to play other games in the series.

There are also many, many other Pokémon games available if you aren't interested in RPGs. There are Pokémon puzzle games, Pokémon fighting games, and Pokémon pinball games. There is even a popular series called *Pokémon Snap* that is all about finding Pokémon in different environments and taking photos of them.

Pokémon characters such as Lucario have become mainstays in the *Super Smash Bros.* series.

Pokémon GO became a worldwide phenomenon shortly after its release, with large crowds gathering in real life to battle each other and try to collect rare Pokémon.

Pokémon characters also show up in other popular Nintendo series, such as *Super Smash Bros.* And of course, there's the wildly popular mobile game *Pokémon GO*, which allows players to walk around the real world and catch new Pokémon using their phones. In other words, your choices are almost endless if you want to try a Pokémon game.

CHAPTER 3

Catch 'Em All

The tagline of the Pokémon series is "Gotta catch 'em all!" Catching new Pokémon is a big part of every game. For each new species you find, you will unlock another entry in your Pokédex. This is like a Pokémon encyclopedia your Pokémon trainer character carries around. The ultimate goal is always to complete the entire Pokédex. This is easier said than done.

Generation one had 151 different Pokémon species to catch, which seemed like a huge number at the time. But today, there are more than 1,000 different Pokémon, and more new species are added with each generation. In the lead-up to each game's release, fans eagerly learn as much as they can about every new Pokémon.

Catching Pokémon is a simple process. First, you need to find a wild Pokémon. Much of your time in each Pokémon game will be spent wandering around different outdoor environments, from green forests to snowy mountain peaks. Each type of environment is home to different Pokémon species, just like how different animals can be found in different environments in real life. Some types of Pokémon can only be found at certain times of day. Others can only be found in

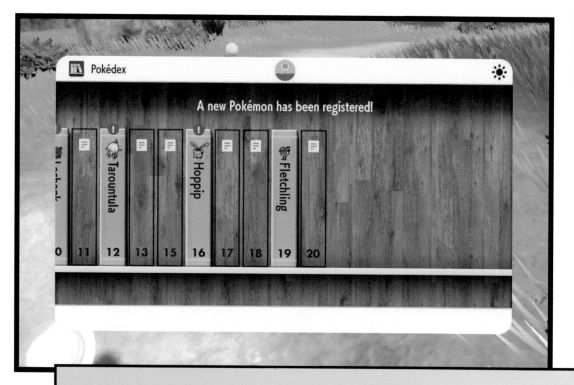

Filling in the Pokédex is one of the most satisfying parts of any Pokémon game.

certain parts of the environment. For example, some only live in water, while others hang out in tall grass.

In older Pokémon games, you will randomly meet Pokémon as your move through wild areas, suddenly kicking off a battle. In newer games, you can see the Pokémon moving around the world, then choose

In newer Pokémon games, you can hunt specific Pokémon types by sneaking up on them and attacking from a distance.

You are challenged by Pokémon Trainer Nemona!

Battling against fellow trainers is a great way to earn money and level up your Pokémon.

whether you want to approach them. Either way, you will eventually end up in battle. You will need to use the Pokémon in your collection to attack the wild Pokémon and lower its health. Be sure not to attack the Pokémon too much—if you cause it to faint, the battle will be over. Once you've lowered the Pokémon's health, you can throw a Poké Ball. This is a special device that can be used to trap a Pokémon inside.

Gotcha!
Rookidee was caught!

Classic red-and-white Poké Balls will serve you well in the early areas of most Pokémon games, but you'll need to upgrade as you get further into your adventure.

If the Poké Ball is successful, the wild Pokémon will be added to your collection. You will be able to raise the Pokémon and use it in battles. However, Poké Balls do not always work on the first try. Some Pokémon are tougher to catch than others. You might need to use more powerful Poké Balls to capture these creatures.

Some Pokémon cannot be captured in the wild. They can only be acquired through other techniques. For example, some Pokémon **evolve** from other species when certain conditions are met. They might turn into new species when they reach a certain level. Others evolve when you give them certain items. For example, if you let Pikachu hold an item called a Thunderstone, it will evolve into Raichu.

Congratulations! Your Wooper evolved into Clodsire!

You might be surprised when one of your favorite Pokémon suddenly evolves at the end of a battle.

Other types of Pokémon can only be found by **breeding** your Pokémon together. Male and female Pokémon of certain species can create eggs together. These eggs can then hatch into new Pokémon. Breeding works differently in different Pokémon games.

In modern Pokémon games, you can trade with random players online. This is a great way to get rid of spare Pokémon that you aren't using.

Home Sweet Home

With so many different Pokémon spread across different games on different systems, trading all your Pokémon from one generation to the next can be complicated. To help make this easier for dedicated Pokémon players, Nintendo has created special apps that allow people to upload their Pokémon from each game. Then they can download the collected Pokémon into newer games using the same app. The first version of the app was called Pokémon Bank. It was released in 2014. In 2020, Pokémon Bank was replaced with a new app called Pokémon Home. The plan is for all newer Pokémon games in the future to keep supporting the app, allowing players to keep transferring their collections of Pokémon for as long as they keep playing the series.

And of course, you can also get new Pokémon by trading with other players. Unlike the first Pokémon games, newer games in the series do not require players to link their game systems together with cables. Instead, you can simply trade with friends over the internet. That means trading is easier than ever!

CHAPTER 4

Battle Strategies

So what's the point of collecting all those Pokémon? For many players, collecting is just the first step to something more fun: battling. Advanced Pokémon players love training their Pokémon carefully to unlock the perfect set of skills, and then combining their well-trained Pokémon to create the perfect team.

You can only carry a certain number of active Pokémon with you at a time when you set off to explore in a Pokémon game. The rest are stored away. Each Pokémon has a few skills it can choose from during battles. As your Pokémon gets stronger, it will learn new skills. You can choose whether to replace an older skill with one of these new ones or simply forget the new skill. This all means that to create a well-balanced team, you will need to choose each Pokémon's skills carefully, and then make sure your team has Pokémon that will work well together.

Each Pokémon has a "type." For example, some are electric type. Others are fire type. These types are either strong, weak, or neutral against various other types. This affects how effective your Pokémon's attacks are and how much damage attacks do to your Pokémon.

Try to build a party of Pokémon with different skills, strengths, and weaknesses.

For example, fire-type Pokémon are strong against ice-type Pokémon. This means if you use a fire-type Pokémon, its fire attacks will do extra damage against ice-type opponents. The opponent's ice attacks will do less damage against your fire-type Pokémon. However, fire-type Pokémon are weak to water-type Pokémon. Their attacks will do less damage, and they will take more damage from opponents. Choosing the right type of Pokémon is the most important part of most battles.

Once you have battled a Pokémon type, future battles against the type will show you whether your attacks will be effective or not.

Stats for each of your Pokémon can be viewed from the game's menu screen.

Pokémon all have **stats** that explain their various strengths and weaknesses. For example, the attack stat tells you how strong a Pokémon's physical attacks will be. Defense tells you how well the Pokémon can defend against physical attacks.

The actual process of battling in a Pokémon game is very simple. When it is your turn, you simply choose which skill you want your Pokémon to use that round. Or, instead, you can also choose to swap out your Pokémon for a different one on your team or use an item from your bag. Once you have made your choice, your Pokémon and your opponent's Pokémon will take turns completing the actions you selected. Which side goes first in a round is determined by the Pokémon's speed stat.

Special Techniques

Aside from damage, you also need to keep an eye out for attacks that cause status effects. For example, some attacks can cause your Pokémon to fall asleep. This can prevent them from acting for several rounds. Or a Pokémon can become confused, making it attack itself from time to time. Some skills can also change a Pokémon's stats temporarily, such as decreasing its defense. Learning to use these kinds of skills alongside your most powerful attacks is an important part of advanced strategy.

As a Pokémon takes damage, its health meter decreases. Once the meter reaches zero, the Pokémon will faint and be removed from the battle. You can heal your Pokémon during a battle using certain skills or by using items in your trainer's bag. The battle ends when all of one side's Pokémon have fainted.

Battling is an important part of capturing new Pokémon in the wild. It's also an essential part of completing the storyline of each game. You'll need to defeat all kinds of powerful Pokémon trainers and other enemies as you play. But for many Pokémon fans, the real fun comes from challenging other players online.

No matter how you like to play, there's always something new to do and learn in the world of Pokémon. So get out there and start capturing your own team of colorful creatures. You'll be a top trainer in no time!

It's time to head out and start exploring the world of Pokémon!

GLOSSARY

breeding (BREE-ding) the process of selecting animals to mate and produce offspring

development (dih-VEL-uhp-muhnt) the process of making video games or other computer programs

evolve (i-VOLV) to change over time

generation (jen-uh-RAY-shuhn) a group of things created as the next version of a previous group

roleplaying games (ROHL-play-ing GAYMZ) games in which the player builds and strengthens a character or set of characters

species (SPEE-sheez) a group of living things that are able to produce offspring with each other

stats (STATS) numerical measurements of different strengths and weaknesses

FIND OUT MORE

Books

Gregory, Josh. *Careers in Esports*. Ann Arbor, MI: Cherry Lake Publishing, 2021.

Loh-Hagan, Virginia. *Video Games. In the Know: Influencers and Trends*. Ann Arbor, MI: 45th Parallel Press, 2021.

Orr, Tamra. *Video Sharing. Global Citizens: Social Media*. Ann Arbor, MI: Cherry Lake Press, 2019.

Reeves, Diane Lindsey. *Do You Like Getting Creative? Career Clues for Kids*. Ann Arbor, MI: Cherry Lake Press, 2023.

Websites

With an adult, learn more online with these suggested searches.

The Official Pokémon Website
Keep up to date with all of the latest Pokémon news at the series' official website.

Bulbapedia
You'll find detailed information about all of the Pokémon games at this fan-created wiki site.

INDEX